# ROBOTS FEEL NOTHING WHEN THEY HOLD HANDS

Written by **ALEC SULKIN**, **ARTIE JOHANN**, and **MICHAEL DESILETS**
Illustrated by **JOE VAUX** and **DOMINIC BIANCHI**
Foreword by **SETH MACFARLANE**, creator of *Family Guy*

CHRONICLE BOOKS
SAN FRANCISCO

Library of Congress Cataloging-in-Publication Data:

Sulkin, Alec.
Robots feel nothing when they hold hands / written by Alec Sulkin, Mike Desilets,
and Artie Johann; illustrated by Joe Vaux and Dominic Bianchi.
    p. cm.
  ISBN 978-0-8118-7883-8
1.  American wit and humor.  I. Desilets, Mike. II. Johann, Artie. III. Vaux, Joe. IV.
Bianchi, Dominic. V. Title.

  PN6165.S89 2012
  818'.60208--dc23

                        2011051333


Manufactured in the United States of America
Designed by Michael Morris

10 9 8 7 6 5 4 3 2 1

Chronicle Books LLC
680 Second Street
San Francisco, California 94107
www.chroniclebooks.com

# A NOTE ABOUT ALEC SULKIN:
## FRIEND, ASSHOLE, LEADER OF THE PACK

### SETH MACFARLANE

When Alec Sulkin asked me to write the foreword to his book, I was honored. It has always been my dream to compose a preface for a collection of reprinted one-liners that can be accessed on the Internet with little or no effort whatsoever. But after getting the initial anti-Semitic grumblings out of my system, I remembered that Alec is my very close friend, the two of us not only having worked on *Family Guy* together for eight-plus years, but also having fought together in Iraq (replace "fought" in the previous sentence with "smoked weed" and "Iraq" with "Studio City").

There are a number of humorous Twitterers in the online community today, but Alec deserves the credit for taking the format and stylizing it in a way that has been adopted by numerous other comedy writers, myself included. What Frank Sinatra did for the long-playing record album, Norman Lear did for the half-hour sitcom, and Rob Schneider did for the awful motion picture, Alec has done for the Twitter feed. As a physically frail man who despises hard work, Alec was the perfect person to take a format that requires small, nine-second bursts of typing at seven-hour intervals, and make it his own. If this book is a success, I truly believe Alec will one day write entire paragraphs, and perhaps even full pages. But for now, enjoy this collection of self-loathing little thought-queefs emitted by a man who is without question one of the most talented comedy writers in Hollywood. His observational skills are superbly augmented by a brain that analyzes, processes, and cross-indexes with the power of a comedy supercomputer to craft hilarious commentaries on even the most mundane topics. And all seemingly without effort. Fuckin' asshole.

*Robots Feel Nothing When They Hold Hands* came together at the offices of *Family Guy* after a couple of guys heard that these other guys were writing jokes on this Internet thing called Twitter. Slowly, a relationship formed. Like all other humans unable to convey emotion, they let the machines do it for them, 140 characters at a time. The guys passed each other every day in the hallway, exchanging silent compliments while motioning toward their respective phones as if to say, "That was a good joke you did while you were in the bathroom shitting." Eventually, work and life just became time in between tweets. And then, finally, the day came when verbal confirmation of what was happening had to be made. The conversation went something like this:

"Hey. This is fun. We should make a book or something."

"Okay."

And now we're here. Three guys who grew up idolizing things like *The Gashlycrumb Tinies* and *The Far Side* get to write a book of their own. Learned human emotion says that the correct response to such exciting news is "joy." The robotic response to such news is "0100110001." Our response is somewhere between "joy" and "0100110001." Stuck in a hybrid human-robot emotional purgatory. But it's not our fault. We're from a generation of do-nothings; the first from an era of people who had everything done for them. Computers did our homework, while movies and television did the rest. Most people made it out unscathed, but we got lost somewhere in between.

Our book is broken down into chapters the only way we know how to break things down: by using things we've seen on TV. Famous people laugh and cry for us, so we don't have to. In fact, we heard that in twenty years, regular people won't even exist anymore. Instead, they'll have become so useless that they'll be reduced to a crude flesh paste that can be gathered up, melted down, and made into racquetballs for the famous.

We chose *Robots Feel Nothing When They Hold Hands* as the title of our book because (1) it will please our eventual robot overlords, and (2) we think it best reflects how we live. We're all being led by a cold, strong hand on a slow, analytical walk through life, forever marching forward toward some place yet TBD. We don't know where we're going; we're just glad we get to see boobs and take drugs on the way.

And remember, we don't want to be your friend. Nobody does. We just want you to laugh.

Signed,

Authors #1–3.

It's amazing that before Facebook we used to have to stare at clocks and windows and shit.

# KURT COBAIN

**KURT COBAIN** was the reluctant voice of a generation and leader of the grunge movement (otherwise known as "noise from the '90s"). He wore flannel, he did drugs, and he was the best singer-songwriter of his time. Unfortunately, he was also the best at shooting himself in the face. In the end, he decided he'd rather be dead than famous. An attitude we wish more people would adopt today.

Still unsure who I hate more: myself or everyone else. Thanks for keeping it close, everyone else.

Keep your friends close and your kinda friends farther away.

With age comes significantly fewer trophies.

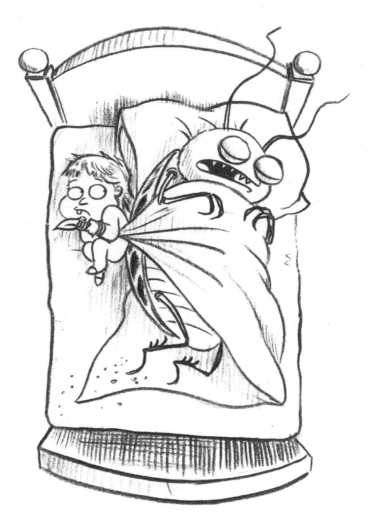

"Don't let the bedbugs bite."
"Okay. Or, as a parent, you could rid my bed of pestilence."

I'd watch a "Where Are They Now?" about kids who could suck their own dicks in high school.

No human is strong enough to resist trying on a wacky hat.

Whenever I feel down, I like to picture a sharply dressed ape calmly sorting through a Rolodex.

A slight wave of the hand in front of an automatic door enhances the illusion that I have the Force.

Imagine the disappointment of future species when they uncover the remains of doormen.

An orchestra conductor is basically a guy who takes a shitload of credit for pushing the "play" button.

Dinner with relatives is like a three hour version of being held under water a half-second too long.

Either sunsets or potato chips are making me fat.
May never figure it out.

Led Zeppelin sounds best in cars that smell like cigarettes.

# Watching a band load their gear into a van is one of life's little equalizers.

Two hundred years ago, joggers would have been institutionalized.

Human vulnerability is never more apparent than when there's no hot water.

Hey, Pink Floyd: Cheer up. You're rock stars.

"Hey, do you wanna play tennis?"
"No. I don't really enjoy looking like a white asshole."

There is nothing funny about a burn victim.
Unless his name happens to be Bernie.

Replacing the words *Strawberry Fields Forever* with
*Beverly Hills Chihuahua* is sadly catchy.

I'm never happier than when I hear somebody slip
and fall in a bathtub.

## "I get all my news from the *Daily Show*,"
said the least original person at the party.

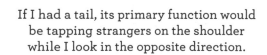

If I had a tail, its primary function would be tapping strangers on the shoulder while I look in the opposite direction.

Weird how a city like Los Angeles, which has so many atheists, also has the best weather.

# SAM NEILL

When looking for a crew of friends, you should always have three types of people: A bully (to protect you from other people), a sober guy (to drive you places), and a dinosaur guy (to help you during the inevitable dinosaur de-extinction). **SAM NEILL** is our source for everything sciencey. Oh, and he also played Damien in one of the *Omen* movies, which means he's down with the devil, and that's pretty cool.

I'm glad people can't see my blank stare
on the other side of their hug.

I'm so tired that I almost forgot our bodies get thrown
in a hole or burned when we die.

Remember, kids, every day after seventeen gets
a little bit worse.

Wow, that black lipstick really brings out the flaws
in your personality.

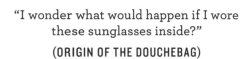

"I wonder what would happen if I wore these sunglasses inside?"

**(ORIGIN OF THE DOUCHEBAG)**

The Great Depression was made way worse by the
fact that there was no TV.
"I'm depressed. What's on TV?"
"Nothing. Not invented yet."

"Hey, wanna dance to 'Jeremy'?"
(*Sigh.*) "Yeah, fine."
(Reason #27 the '90s sucked)

I may be at my happiest while watching "this sports team is
getting better" montages.

Whenever I read romantic poetry, I like to think the author
wrote it while taking a dump.

A good way to make or break a friendship is to show up with a tandem bike.

If God wanted us to floss, it'd be in the Bible.

It wouldn't kill them to say
"no, thanks" to drugs.

Great film about the Armenian war effort:
*Uncommon Velour.*

If you think seeing someone pick their butt and smell it
is gross, try seeing someone pick their butt and listen to it.

# OTIS NIXON

**OTIS NIXON** is a former Major League Baseball player. He holds the illustrious title of the only guy in baseball history to ever end a World Series on a bunt groundout. He also once missed an entire World Series because he got suspended for using cocaine. I guess for the most part Otis Nixon is culturally insignificant. Though if there's anything to be learned from him, it's that people can achieve mild and forgettable success.

Tipsy Irish cops seem like quaint characters in the movies, but you know they killed a lotta black guys.


Some people go their whole lives without ever knowing what's wrong with Seal's face.

If you forget a girl's name, "Heyyyy, you look great!" is always an adequate substitute.

Once or twice a year, it's okay to pretend
your legs are lady legs.

Prove that lightning isn't wizards fighting. You can't.

You never want to be described as the girl who "really went to town on that cake."

"Wow, she's got a great . . . softball body," said the man who couldn't lie.

It's not really a public rest room unless
people can watch you go.

When in doubt, melt cheese on it.

A high-waisted post-shower towel wrap instantly transforms me into a '50s muscle man.

"Do Not Enter" signs could also just say, "Quirky-Funny Women Dancing and Making Goofy Faces."

If I could travel back in time, I would lower body-image standards.

The phrase "I think we need another minute" exists only because of women.

Imagine when the first guy walked into a room with a powdered wig on. That would have been a fun room to be really stoned in.

Ben Franklin looks like a Founding Lesbian.

# "SULLY" SULLENBERG

**"SULLY" SULLENBERG** is the hero pilot who courageously landed a passenger jet on the Hudson River, saving the lives of all aboard. He takes shits, too. Not just like hero shits, but long, sweaty, pray-to-God ones too. And he picks weird food from his teeth, and his wife probably fantasizes about a life with a different man. They all do. Just saying. The hero stripped of his deed is just us, and we suck. Also, he did crash a plane.

"Women will speak to no end of minor achievements."
**(EARLY NOSTRADAMUS PREDICTION)**

"Hang on, let me just tie the sleeves of my denim shirt around
my waist. Then we can skadoodle."
**('90S MOM TWEET)**

Some people look like they've been slowly pulled
out of their own shower drain.

Wait, so you're saying a single woman in her forties is having an exhibition of her photography? Where?!

Always a bridesmaid, never not hungry.

Remember, there is no "we" in "I."

Guys with ponytails don't care what the rest of us think, which is good, because we think they suck.

Hey, adults: Let's let kids have the word *tummy*.
We don't need it.

"Et tu, Brute?"
"Yeah, et fucking me, asshole."
**(WORDS AFTER FAMOUS LAST WORDS #2)**

Real courage is pre-1900 cunnilingus.

I think the Venn diagram guy just liked
watching circles fuck.

Alcohol does not make your problems go away. It just turns them into rock songs for a few hours.

An automatic toilet prematurely flushing is like a waiter pulling your plate before you've finished your fries.

I know that I will always hesitate before using another man's soap.

"Yes, she's very ill. The doctor said she'll be confined
to a one-piece for the rest of her life."

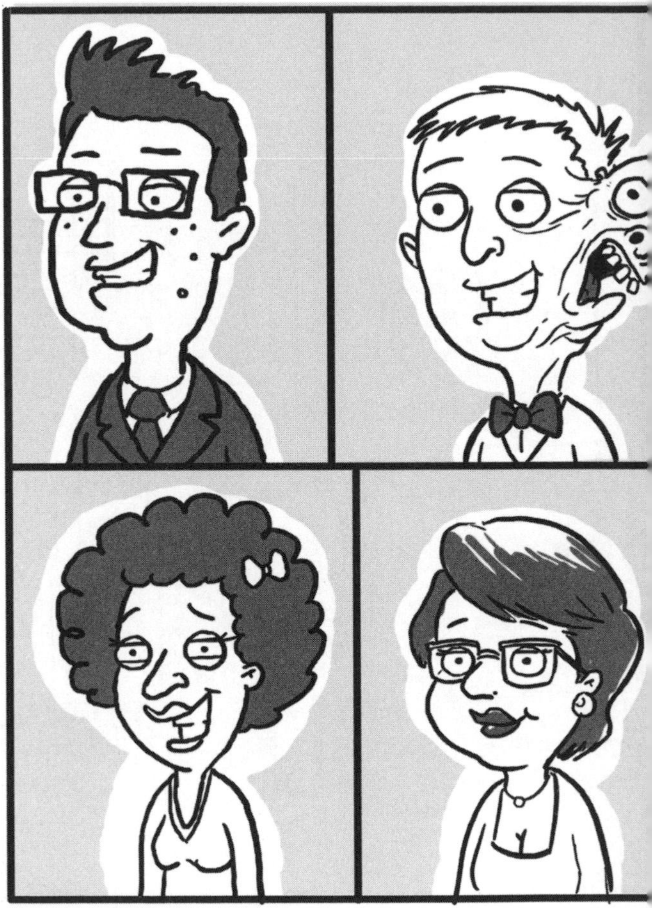

You never wanna be known as "the weird guy with the head."

"Jesus. It smells like someone's dad took a shit in here."

There's no right way for a straight man to light a candle, put on ChapStick, or look at his fingernails.

He cums on her.
**(PORNO SPOILER ALERT)**

A hangover is always a little better when accompanied by the vague memory of fucking.

When a girl refers to a guy as "an old friend," that generally means they've boned. (P.S. The guy is not your friend.)

If your father is torn between the fig salad and the Dover sole, your father is gay.

Life is so much easier if you like burgers.

That sounds delicious, but may I just get mine in a bowl? The word *terrine* makes me feel like we're all trying too hard.

Look, if nothing hit your underwear, you didn't shit your pants. You just crapped in your ass. No worries.

In a Western, you don't wanna be one of the three guys.
You wanna be the one guy.

**HOROSCOPE FOR GUYS NAMED LANE:**
You seek a decent pickup basketball game. It's okay to
wear a T-shirt; it's the weekend. Don't trust Cory.

Watching an old woman feel passion in any way makes me ill.

"I'm just in a weird place right now," said the man in a Slavic family's house.

Bug-eyed people, just look down.
We'll come get you if we need you.

"Let me just run it by the ol' ball and ball."
—Married gay guys

"So, I have tickets to a play.
It's about—"
"Stop. Nope."

Let's hold off calling dolphins the smartest animal until they
stop getting caught in nets.

Winos are the Jewish guys of the alcoholic world.

# DOC HOLLIDAY

**DOC HOLLIDAY** was a drinker, a gambler, and an outlaw. He took what he wanted and fucked when he felt like it. In other words, he had a mustache and he knew how to use it.

Can't tell if there's a mosquito in the room or just faraway Bee Gees music.

"Dude, watch out! There's two guys wearing masks behind you!"

(Pitcher Gets Amnesia, Warns Batter)

"Do you want one of these cookies?"
"No, thanks. I'm an adult."

Drunk sex is like listening to "Sweet Caroline" without the "Sweet Caroline" part of the song ever coming on.

Woman on deathbed:
"Tell me . . . I lived a good life."
Her husband:
"I'm sorry, I can't. You were a crossing guard for thirty-five years."

Easy, *Matrix*-coat guy.

I hate it when people get depressed and blame it on the seasons. It's not winter's fault you're a loser.

"My dog totally thinks he's a person."
"No, you think he's a person, and people think you're pathetic."

No need to wipe if you're just jumping right into the pool.

White guys don't care who knows that they just shit.

## JCIMH!!!
—Pervert IM shorthand for "Just Came in My Hand!!!"

When did milk go from a delicious morning friend to a maniac who punches his way out of my asshole?

Good things come
to those who wait,
except for those
who wait for
the bus.

Sex in a bathroom doesn't count as "making love." You just got banged amid filth.



If I had to be stuck on a desert island with one thing, I'd choose a chair. I might be starving to death, but at least I'm not standing.



Classified ad with comedic potential:
**RECENT AMPUTEE SEEKS ARMS DEALER.**

"Okay, say 'Mmmmm.'"
(Photographer to a kid with really big gums)

"Dude, would you fuck Hawaii?"
"Nah. Her i's are too close together."

From now on, if something is boring, it's "parent-sex."

"Open on: An office filled with happy women
who enjoy working together."
**(SCI-FI SCRIPT)**

I guess we're still
waiting for that
thank-you
note from horses
for inventing cars.

"Oh my God!"

(Any girl after the first bite of any dessert anywhere)

There's definitely a type of girl who can be summed
up simply with "no dad."

Boy, in HD you can really see the crowd not chanting "Rudy!"

If I'd been a cowboy, I would've been very good at lightly
grabbing the brim of my hat as a lady passed. That's it.

# TARZAN

**TARZAN** is a man of few words and a confused but powerful sense of sexuality. Also, he lived with a family of apes and never once had his face ripped off by them. Plus, having a family of apes really simplifies gift-giving around the holidays: bunches of bananas were always a big hit.

I'm gonna suggest we change the beeping sound when big trucks back up to a gay guy saying "Move, move, move . . . "

When someone invites you over, rub their ear and say, "Looking forward to it." That way, they won't be disappointed when you don't show.

Proudly urinating with my hands on my hips
is the closest I'll come to feeling like a superhero.

Just once I'd like to give myself that "serial killer about to move to a new town" haircut in the mirror.

Prius: Because sometimes a shitty personality just isn't enough.

If a person prefaces something with "I never do this, but . . . ," they do that shit all the time.

I can tell by your eyebrows that you're quite hairy.

Can't we just give people with Parkinson's disease a
tambourine to lighten the mood?

My mailman isn't really mine, is he?

I like to call classier hand jobs "penicures."

Owning a piano is like having a really cool gay guy who just hangs out in your living room all the time.

If these walls could talk, they'd probably say something about where I've been wiping my boogers.

Sex beats blow job.
Blow job beats hand job.
Hand job beats masturbation.
Masturbation beats off.

"Hold on. I'm just gonna go use my hand, then my mouth, to see what's going on under that cow."
**(THE ORIGIN OF MILK)**

You know what's cool? Surfing. You know what's not? Surfers.

I wonder if black guys call the board game Sorry! "My Bad!"

"So long, suckers."
—Exit sign at lollipop factory

I can never hear the ocean when I put a seashell up to my ear.
It's always just a guy named Bernard drowning.

"You wear the mark of a pussy."
—Olden-times bully

Masturbating with my pinky finger extended is the closest I'll ever get to being a randy English gentleman.

You guys, this is gross, but I sucked my mom's tits.

*Lord of the Rings* seems like kind of a racist book. I mean, it doesn't even have one Tolkien black guy.

If you're put on the invite list only after the phrase **"Now, who am I forgetting?"** you're not making your mark as a human.

Getting a salad at McDonald's is like playing
footsie with a hooker.

# If you had a pool as a kid, people didn't really like you for you.

Pooping without touching the seat shall now be known as
"Pitching from the stretch."

My posture can be best described as "third guy in the evolution of man."

Revenge is never sweeter than when it's taken on somebody's toothbrush.

# JEAN-CLAUDE VAN DAMME

**JEAN-CLAUDE VAN DAMME** often fought robots, but you had to wonder, was he himself one, and was his directive to save the world with black jeans and hybrid karate? Also, Belgium in the house?

When did the office kitchen become more frightening than breathing sounds from a dark basement?

"Get out of my dreams, get into my van with the tinted windows and the Native American mural . . . fucking now!"

Old black people should be allowed to cut in line.
They've been through enough shit.

I think all orgies should kick off with a cannon shot.
That way, no one looks stupid if they start early.

Fat guys, everybody knows the black T-shirt trick by now.
You can't hide anymore.

Come on, Delaware. Do something.

———

Sleeping in my childhood bed is like driving
a Big Wheel to work.

**A SOUND THAT MAY PLAY ON LOOP IN HELL:**
someone unsuccessfully closing a glove box.

January 4th, and the push-ups have already stopped.

Birds don't even know it's Friday. Idiots.

I would have called the Internet "numbers and letters and pictures world."

# Nothin' creepier than a white guy in a white van.

Don't make fun of old people. They have really thin skin.

"Smarter than your average bear" is not saying much. An average bear can't even hold a fork.

I wish there were a time machine just to send spoiled
L.A. kids back to World War II.

Girls loudly reacting to text messages
is the new nails-on-a-chalkboard.

The first half hour of my day is spent lying in bed, winning fake arguments in my head.

# Going to the DMV is like standing before wiping. Sometimes you don't have a choice.

Still having porn on the screen is the male version of leaving the iron on.

Nothing stops me in my tracks like a big swig from the wrong can of soda.

# AMELIA EARHART

**AMELIA EARHART** was an aviation pioneer and American icon. Also, ladies . . . she got lost. Let's admit it. She got totally lost.

SIDE NOTE: Hilary Swank played Amelia Earhart in the movie *Amelia*.

SIDE NOTE TO THE SIDE NOTE: Hilary Swank shows her tits in the movie *Boys Don't Cry*.

No matter how thin I get, I'll always subtly make sure
I'm on the "shirts" team.

I feel like enough stuff has happened
for a *We Didn't Start the Fire 2*.

I think we should start calling unathletic white guys "matzos."

"Don't worry, I'll hold your stuff. You just worry about making friends."
—Cargo shorts

One of life's equalizers:
Those real mean girls in high school had
kids earlier than they wanted.

"Hey, world! You suck!"
(BOSTON GUY SPACE WALK)

"Guys, I know she's not that hot, but darn it all, she makes me laugh."

(THINGS MEN NEVER SAY #6)

"Hang on, I might wanna stay here a while. This guy's quoting *Holy Grail*."

(WHAT PEOPLE WHO QUOTE PYTHON HOPE OTHERS THINK)

# "And for those of you looking for extra credit ..."
## (PHRASES THAT TURN MY BRAIN OFF #12)

If I were a coroner, I'd probably just write "brain broke" instead of "aneurism," because it's easier to spell.

To rival the guys brushing their teeth in the men's room, I'm gonna be the guy casually putting on a condom.

"I'll wait for the next one."
—Procrastinating lifeguard

"We can beat Off. We have beat Off.
But we need to keep beating Off!"
(Start-up mosquito-repellent company exec rallying support)

If I were a plumber, I'd set up shop in Africa and re-label
myself "Shit and Water God."

If former president James Garfield looked more like Garfield the Cat, I would know a lot more about his time in office.

Just took a dump that was like barely getting a
couch through a dorm room door.

Latina women, please calm down.
Everyone's trying to enjoy themselves.

If I were a scientist, I would have deduced that the
wind is a horde of jogging ghosts.

The belly button had quite a precipitous fall from "provider of sustenance" to "body garbage can."

Sometimes I'll grab someone's ankle under the bathroom stall and scream, "You're shitting wrong!"

Somewhere, some asshole can't believe that it's already Thanksgiving.

Smiling women wielding glasses of white wine scare the shit out of me.

.

Bread crumbs.
Bread crumbs.
Bread crumbs.

(DUCK GROCERY LIST)

Let's just retire the phrase "It puts hair on your chest."
Nobody wants that anymore.

"I'm tastin' some fuckin' beans or something."
—Low-class guy at wine tasting

"Whaddaya think, your piss don't stink?!"
(Asparagus to broccoli)

Though Tyrannosaurus rex has perfect arms for carrying trays, it lacks the patience needed to be a good waiter.

Call funny girls pretty and pretty girls funny. Thank me in the morning.

I hope my last words aren't
## "I'll clean that jizz up tomorrow."

When I die, don't put me in a coffin. Put me in ten separate shoe boxes and hide them at a Payless shoe store of your choosing.

Love means never having to hold in that gross Chinese-food fart.

"Wanna listen to Cat Stevens?"
"No, I'm just gonna almost-sneeze for thirty-five minutes. That should do it."

Russia just seems like a whole country of Pittsburgh.

I was depressed for like eleven years, but then a distant cousin sent me a virtual card.

# GAETAN DUGAS

Look familiar? Hope not, because **GAETAN DUGAS** is patient zero for AIDS. This French Canadian airline steward flew from city to city gay sexing a disease into existence. It was just like the movie *Outbreak* but with penises. Apparently, he was told that he was sick and yet continued to bravely have gay sex. There's a soulless disregard for humanity that only a robot would understand.

Local commercials remind us all that everywhere is terrible.

My smile is like an ill-fitting blazer I put on for company.

**(LITTLE-KNOWN AMERICAN FACTS #41)**
Gary, Indiana, was founded as a direct response to the
founding of Ron, Ohio.

"That guitar sounds great. Let's play twelve of them at the same time."

(SOUTH AMERICAN BAND MEETING)

It's better to
have loved
and lost than
to be the dad
at the beach
with really big
nipples.

Little-known Civil War fact: In high school, the South was voted most likely to secede.

Ginger ale is like the former president of a company who's now just a respected consultant.

Repeatedly whispering my own name in a pitch-black room really waters my crazy-garden.

I'm creating a new texture. It's called
"fat through a hammock."

**FACT:**
Every male you know has inadvertently
gotten cum on you somehow.


I want a picture so big that I can't tell where TV ends
and life begins.


Sleeping may be dying practice.

"Some will think this week is going by slowly, while others will say that it's flying by."
(EARLY NOSTRADAMUS PREDICTION)

According to the U.S. Census Bureau, 89 percent of men over 6'3" are assholes.

I heard Godzilla was just looking for a bathroom.

"Oh, man. You people have no idea how wacky my socks are."

—Inner monologue of the wacky sock wearer

When you eat
an apple, you're
eating a tree's
balls.

I bet some of the dumber wolves howl at the sun.

**DRIVING TIP #8:**
When on the highway, be wary of Jaguars.
They're generally driven by the near-dead.

After extensive research, I've concluded that the grossest sound the human body can make is a tub-fart in two inches of water.

1:34: The point in the night when a single guy realizes that nobody cares.

My solution to the energy crisis? Invent a device that harnesses the energy created by toothless people rolling their lips.

A "bachelorette" sash is a good way to let everybody know that tonight you might give a no-look hand job.

I've never said "I miss you, too," and meant it.

If I saw the world as Keanu Reeves did in *The Matrix*, everything would just be Internet porn categories.

If you accidentally make eye contact with a dude while you're dancing, that means you danced with that dude for a second.

If you can convince someone to get in your trunk, you get to keep them.

# JOHN F. KENNEDY

**JOHN F. KENNEDY** is not the John F. Kennedy you're thinking of. This John F. Kennedy is a guy I went to high school with who just happens to share the same name as one of our former presidents. This John F. Kennedy is an accountant in Arkansas or something. I just remember him from school because he was the kid with the same name as the president, and also the kid who shit himself at a middle-school dance.

"I kinda feel like surrounding myself with chatty,
enthusiastic women tonight."

I doubt I'd fuck even the best-looking octopus.

If you're a man over forty, and you're pissed that people forgot your birthday, you're off the team.

Camels look like they might lie to each other sometimes.

Let's all keep an eye on Tilda Swinton. She may be here on Earth to do something weird.

Why aren't there novelty toilets? It'd be pretty cool to burn one atop a lion.

"Hurry the fuck up."
**(GENERAL GUY TO GIRL NOTE)**

"Hey, do you wanna stink, shit in a hole, and get really damp at night?"

(Do you want to go camping?)

Toilet paper is a poor substitute for a beach towel.

"Out with the
dead, in with
the old."

—Nursing homes

"Is that leaf poisonous?" "I don't know. I live in a house. There's TV there."

"Have some fucking dignity." —Other birds to seagulls

I bet there's a dog rivalry between the "woofs" and the "barks."

All nature shows should be called
*Animals Fucking Hate Each Other.*


If I had to eat a human head, I'd probably start with the ear.


## "The Woman and Her Day"
### (TERRIBLE PARABLES #1)

If you don't care
what others think,
I bet there's fewer
than six people
who love you.

When in doubt, do
the opposite
of whatever
the guy in black
jeans does.

The older you get, the harder it is to find a bath buddy.

## "Do you have an innie or an outie?"
## "We talkin' dick or belly button?"

"And your name shall be 'Kris' with a 'K.' You will be like all other Chrises except you will always choose Coors Light over toothpaste."

I think a watchgoose would be more
effective than a watchdog.

It's hard not to look like an asshole while dusting your trophy case.

"What was that noise that just came from your throat?" "Sorry. Tharted."

When Jesus died for our sins, I doubt he thought it would be so guys named Dylan could wear Tevas to brunch.

If God's a girl, I'm in trouble. Sorry, if God exists, I'm in trouble. Thank God he's fake.

# T-1000

**T-1000** is a liquid metal from *Terminator 2*. He has the ability to change into whatever, and whomever, he wants at any time he wants. Which is awesome, because being yourself sucks, but being my neighbor's daughter is awesome. That's who I'd change into, by the way. If I were T-1000, I'd change into my neighbor's daughter and then take a three-hour, curtains open, in-front-of-a-mirror shower.

Can we call throwing up and shitting at the same time
*bi-arrhea*? That'd be fun.

"Quickly, Professor Science-Face!
Engage the neutron simulator!"
(SCRIPT BY GUY WHO'S BAD AT NAMING CHARACTERS)

I'm not one of the religious Jews. I'm one of the
"Guys, guys let's just listen to what the
Nazis have to say" Jews.

I'm convinced that with every salad I eat, I become a less interesting person.

There is no act more graceful than the subtle lift of a man's leg to separate sack from thigh.

Penis to balls: "I guess that's the deferens between you and me."

Dating me is like opening a fancy gift box, only to find a couple of cigarette butts and a half-dead bee inside.

"Hold on a sec. I just gotta adjust my junk."
—Priest's sermon off to a bad start

If I were in charge of naming bones, I would have named our ribs "guts cage."

If I'm ever with my dad when someone asks where I'm from, I just point at his balls.

"And your eternity consists of a life-drawing class where all the models look and act like Ethels."
**(PERSONAL HELL #43)**

Sucks that a lot of fond memories include old guys' laps.

Necrophilia is the nail in the coffin.

In photos with five or more women, there are always two who no longer speak to each other.

Gray hair isn't sophisticated. It means you're dying.

It's gonna be really sad when we start seeing "Grandma just checked in at the cemetery" on Foursquare.

"I love you, Dad. I'm just not 'in love' with you."
**(WEIRD THANKSGIVING #18)**

When you make a call and someone picks up and says, "This is Martin," you know you've dialed the wrong number.

It seems unfair that one of the symptoms of Lou Gehrig's disease isn't being really good at baseball for a few years.

"Oh, this isn't a wedgie. I tuck my pants into my ass because I like the way it looks."

"God, I'm just so exhausted," said every woman in every workplace ever.

A lot of girls who dance on bars
just aren't dance-on-bar hot.

I'm guessing hell is going to be just forty people carefully watching me dance.


If you feel like a dead relative is watching over you, they're not. They're dead.


I'm way more scared of white guys with thick goatees than of any minority.

My wife and I are trying to get pregnant: I leave a little on the toilet seat, and she scoots forward.

Before I put on my pants, I often look at them and whisper, **"I'm about to be inside you."**

**"Good work on the Timmy account."**
—Dad having fun with the way mom handled punishment of son

Your favorite
lake has killed
a couple of kids.

A sound that may play on loop in hell: people singing "Happy Birthday" to a guy named Sal.

WebMD just called me a faggot.

"I'll have the salmon," said the man no one liked.

Next time you're in a boring conversation, just slap your lips, look around, and say, "Fuckin' hungry."

I don't feel bad for the people killed in *Jaws*. When I know where a murderer lives, I don't go swimming in his bathtub.

In church, shouldn't the blood of Christ come with the body? Why do we need to see another guy for that?

# ADAM (OF ADAM AND EVE)

**ADAM** was the only man to experience a world without women. God gave him the earth and dominion over the animal kingdom, and he gave them all away for tits. We understand. Also, there is no God, so the whole thing is kind of a weird, fake lesson created by liars and thieves.

A lot of people get hurt trying to see what
their assholes look like.

When someone says,
## "People grieve in their own way,"
it means someone's grieving like a dick.

The days of wine and roses have become the days of weed
and scratch tickets.

Nothing warms the heart of a lonely woman like a cheap-jewelry sale at work.

I would have called Christopher Columbus "Chris" the whole trip over.

A towel draped over my shoulders always gives me an undeserved sense of triumph.

I enjoy driving
by hair salons
and yelling,
"Nope!"
as people
walk out.

Nothin' says
"I'm not above beating off in my pants"
like a pair of stonewashed jeans.

The icing on the douchebag cake is a money clip.

Kids, befriend a bully. That's the
best advice I can give you.

You can usually tell if a guy has drummed in front of a mirror before.

I love music, so why is the question
**"Wanna hear this song I wrote?"**
one of the worst in the English language?

Well, ladies, it looks like chivalry is gone. But, on the bright side, guys that beat off in their cars are still around.

Sweatpants and
frozen pizza
should thank
each other.

I think it's nice that the vowels sometimes let
Y into their crew.

An Irishman, an Italian, and a Jew walk into a bar. I don't have enough room to describe what happens, but the Jew ends up looking cheap.

"It's a shame. Jim had CEO written all over him. He just had to throw that football at the company picnic."

**(THROWS LIKE A GIRL CASUALTY #6)**

"Here, try a sip."
"No, thanks. Your mouth is gross as shit."